Time and Tide

Rob Kersley

Rob Kersley

Copyright © Rob Kersley 2023

The right of Rob Kersley to be identified as the author of this work has been asserted in accordance with sections 77 and 78 of the Copyright Design and Patent Act 1988.

Email: rlkersley@aol.co.uk

Published by ArtNut imprint of MA Publisher (Penzance)
Email: mapublisher@yahoo.com
Website: www.mapublisher.org.uk
Released on January 2023

Print on Demand, printed in United Kingdom

ISBN-13: 978-1-910499-95-5

All rights reserved. No part of this publication may be reproduced, stored in a retrieval system, or transmitted, in any form or by any means, electronic, mechanical, photocopying, recording, public performances or otherwise, without prior written permission of the copyright holder, except for brief quotations embodied in critical articles or reviews.

Disclaimer:
All expressions and opinions of the work belong to the artists/Author and MAP & ArtNut does not share or endorse any other than to provide the open platform to publish their work. For further information on MAP policies please email: mapublisher@yahoo.com for further information and submission guidelines.

Cover designed by Mayar Akash
Cover image: by Rob Kersley (Penzance, Cornwall)
Copy edit: Liz Kersley
Typeset in Times Roman

 Paper printed on is FSC Certified, lead free, acid free, buffered paper made from wood-based pulp. Our paper meets the ISO 9706 standard for permanent paper. As such, paper will last several hundred years when stored.

Dedication

To Liz
Everything for you

Rob Kersley

Contents

Dedication	3
Introduction	7
I'll Be Home For Christmas	9
My Greying Lab	13
31,536,000 Grains	15
Where Is Love	18
Poor Little Rich Kid	21
It's Only A House	23
Before And After	25
Elle Climber	27
Abstinence	29
Escape	31
St Donald & St Nigel	33
The Tragic Garthbrengy Murder	35
Russia 2018	37
Cornish Reflection	39
The River And The Rock	41
Don't Go Near The News Today	43
Hate Criminal	45
Venus	49
The Chocoholic	50
Long In The Tooth	52
When Kipling Discovered Curry	55
Rosa Hubermann	57
Don't Stare Into The Sun	59
James Gatz	61
Amir	65
Polskie Wroble	67
Comrade Corbyn	69
Bishop Myriel	71
London Calling	73
I'll Be Home For Christmas Part 2	75
Sleepless In November	81
Don't Let Go	83
Domestically Abused	85
Time And Space And Trewellard	87
When You Look At Me That Way	91
A Game Of Many Halves	93
Tickled Trout	95
Lamorna	97
Ikeaworld	99

Culture Check	104
Long Rock Landmark	107
The Fast Bubble	109
They Can Come Out Now	112
Tug Of Love	115
Acknowledgements	118
About The Author	119

Introduction

One of the totally unexpected developments from my totally unexpected relocation to the Honddu Valley, was finding a voice. Perhaps I felt fortunate to have survived the sudden termination of the previous chapter and the shockingly helpless unfolding of its ever more difficult pages. The discovery that these were to be the final paragraphs of a marriage born of tender, teenage sweethearts was as abrupt as it was tragic and unexpected. But, out of those ashes of despair and disbelief there was light. Liz came into my life with honesty, pragmatism, tenderness and love. I married Liz and together with my daughter Katherine, moved to Lower Chapel in the Honddu Valley. So, perhaps I felt that a miracle had indeed delivered me safely and that I had nothing to lose. Or, maybe the events of that hideous storm that washed me up, and into a place that was to become so special to me, tenderised or somehow sensitised my consciousness. Either way, it was there in the Honddu Valley that it really began. It was there that broken things were rebuilt. It was there that preconceptions were revisited and it was there that I felt the urge, the absolute necessity to communicate how that process left me feeling.

I began writing a regular blog called The Honddu Valley Herald in 2013 as a means of staying in touch with my good friend Chris Jones after he emigrated to New Zealand. These light-hearted prose evolved from commenting on developments in South Wales, to rugby matches and inevitably to global events. I would mention these correspondences to other friends who would enjoy them and pass them on to others who would then reply to me. Readership numbers therefore increased at a dramatic rate, but as western political ideologies shifted further and further to the populist right, an anxiety developed in me regarding its negative social change and the stubborn denial and inaction regarding our planet's climate crisis. The Honddu Valley Herald then turned from prose to poetry with its delivery less flippant, in an attempt to articulate these deeply held concerns.

The Honddu Valley Herald became a vehicle, a splint, a release valve, an elixir, a platform, a springboard, a highway and a journey. Thank you to everyone who has read, commented, laughed, cried, shared and engaged in these poems.

Time and Tide is the totally unexpected result of the first year or so of Honddu Valley Heralds, and I am both thrilled and grateful to see these early pieces in book form. Thank you.

Rob Kersley

I'll Be Home for Christmas

The warm glow from shop windows as I stroll back up The Hayes,
Crowded streets and crazy, jam-packed stores. It's that time of year again.
Busy plans, happy deadlines, merry chaos, joyous malls,
Gordon's, Riocha, Brains SA ...and paracetamol.

A daze of contactless five card tricks, all running to chase the ace.
SAD condition and chronic winter blues have vanished without a trace.
Mentally ticking off my list, back on the heaving street,
I caught her eye, this foetal young woman. She wasn't shopped off her feet.

Curled up like a kitten on her cardboard bed with stained sleeping bag all about,
I was striding by with bags in hand, done in and all shopped out.
Back through the crowds, her stone grey face, I caught a glimpse once more,
Her vacant stare into vacant space, outside that vacant store.

I denied my selective conscience, just as far as Toys R Us,
Tried to convince myself it's her free choice, if she wants to sleep rough.
But by the time I reached the NCP, I was going back full tilt,
Was this compassion, morbid curiosity or was I driven by some kind of guilt?

I took her a cup of hot chocolate and a handful of paltry silver,
Her tearful gratitude humbled me, said she was too tired and hungry to shiver.
I asked how long she'd been lying there; she pulled her arm out from under her hip,
She glanced at a photo ...then looked away, biting her trembling lip.

She shrugged and stuffed her arms into her armpits; she had dried blood around her mouth,
Said it all went wrong when her mum's new man moved in, and that's when she moved out.
She sniffed and said, *I can't go back, suicidal that would be,*
Then half-coughed, half-sobbed; *I can't believe, that this is happening to me.*

I asked about the photo in her hand. She said, *that's Mum and Dad and me,*
Dad was taken from us before his time. Hit and run near our house in Leigh.
I think me and Mum went into free-fall. I worry about her a lot.
This new guy she's got ...complete psycho, I think she's lost the plot.

She looks again at the photo, *Dad's death was so unfair,*
As she speaks I see she's lost a tooth. I ask, what happened there?
Oh that, that's the psycho's handiwork, didn't like me saying 'no'.
He grabbed my arm but I got away, that's why I can't go home.

cont.

I've got to go, but don't go away. I didn't like leaving her on her own,
I march to a café and search for homeless charities on my phone.
I rang the number, and begged the gentle voice on the other end,
Can you help? She is so vulnerable; she has no family or friends.

We'll try, she said, *but it's Christmas ...you know. I'll see what we can do,*
It's getting worse though every year, not just adults, it's children too.
One hundred and twenty-eight thousand kids without a home this Christmas ...it's bleak.
And around a hundred and forty more families, becoming homeless every week.

What? How? I ask. Where's it going wrong?
Debt? Repossessions? ...The State can't cope, we've known this all along.
They live in hostels, B and B's, temporary accommodation awaited,
This end of the food chain are the suffocated,
The relegated, the relocated and inevitably repudiated.

I ended the call more focused and determined to try to help.
I'll go to Cotswold's, buy her another sleeping bag, the warmest one they sell.
Then I wondered if I should. Is it appropriate, would it offend or not?
I'll ask her first. I left the café, and jogged back to her spot.

She was gone! No sight, no sign of her, just her soggy cardboard bed.
Which way? I darted up and down, my mind was full of dread.
She'd gone, disappeared. But what /who had taken her?
Despondent, I trudged back to the car, the last two hours seemed like a blur.

Driving back over the Beacons. Trance-like, preoccupied and so sad I could have cried.
In my climate controlled car, back to my family, back to my home.
Back to my centrally heated home ...imagine not having a home!
Back to my wife and my family ...imagine being totally alone!

I think of her missing tooth, her smile, dried blood under her nose.
I imagine one hundred and twenty-eight thousand children,
Abandoned, forsaken, dispossessed and still the number grows.
One hundred and forty more families each week, and that's in the UK alone,
I give thanks for the life I find myself in, but question the favouritism shown.

Dropping down from Storey Arms, I turn on the radio to change the context,
But they're playing, The Manics', *If You Tolerate This, Then your Children Will Be Next.*
I change channels and now it's Bing Crosby's, *I'll Be Home for Christmas.*
This has got to be coincidence? ...But even so, it's vicious.

cont.

Suddenly, I'm kicking-off my shoes inside my familiar front door.
Solemnly, I'm walking up the stairs onto the kitchen floor.
Sullenly, I put the shopping down. I answer, Yes, I'm OK.
Actually no, I'm not. How could I be? ...nothing is OK!

I tell my family about that poor homeless girl from Leigh,
Then I tell them what the girl at the homeless charity told me:
That homelessness has doubled in the last seven years alone,
And in that time, our government has made 452 separate announcements,
...As if that will atone!

...But there's never any action,
The homeless don't have influence, so the homeless don't have traction.
So there's never any money,
Never for these people,
And there's never been so many,
And it's never felt so pitiful.

It's never been so one-sided, so greedy and so wrong,
And it's never gonna change until we see beyond our own.
Because, 'Charity Begins at Home' is a myth that undermines
The very meaning of the word that it was once meant to define!

They're all looking at me now and I know I'm making them stare,
But I still see her bloodied nose, her broken tooth and matted hair.

What does it say about you and I
That we let them down this way?
And how will we justify ourselves to God on judgement day?

So we thought we'd have a turkey this year,
We thought we'd make mulled wine.
It dropped down to minus two last night,
But indoors, I'm feeling fine.

But the instinct of this season,
Remains as basic as it seems.
That's why she will be home for Christmas
...If only in her dreams.

Rob Kersley

My Greying Lab

I hold Woody's heavy head gently in my arms,
Tell him, it's ok ...it doesn't matter.
A contented sigh escapes from him,
He knows this is his place, and I know that it's mine.

I hold his noble head in my hands,
Whisper in his velvet ear, not to worry
About his little accident last night.
The loss of dignity doesn't suit him.

To be a creature's entire world,
His master, his keeper, his purpose.
What trust he shows, what an honour he bestows,
This private bond makes no sense to anyone else,
Is this understanding ours alone?

He accepts his achy knees,
And his fading energy these days.
But he doesn't hanker for the past like me.
He tells me to let go of yesterday.
He urges me not to think so much, just to feel ...so I try, but I'm not so brave.

His contentment is an education,
His trust flatters me.
His acceptance, so natural.
All intuition ...the heart, so honest.

When he sleeps, he dreams of the holidays, the journeys, the adventures.
His great paws twitch as he sees his youthful self again,
Trotting through the dew, smelling the new day.
Eyes darting behind closed lids, in his own world,
Cheeks puffing as he barks silently.

I dread the day we lose him,
But he's oblivious of the future.
His innings, like mine is outside his control,
The difference is, he accepts it
And is just grateful of the here and now.

cont.

Rob Kersley

But if I could push the waters back upstream,
If I could stop the sun from rising from the mountains,
If only I could just press pause, and preserve his life, their life, this life.
If only…

My priceless family, my precious friends.
The many I know, the millions I don't.
To preserve the joy, to hold back the pain,.
So we can all stay here forever, like my greying lab,
Then God knows I surely would.

31,536,000 Grains

A second
Is a grain of sand,
A moment,
A glance,
A bird in hand.

A second is a blink of the eye,
A pang,
A peck,
A kiss goodbye.

A second, the finest thread that leaves
A stitch within your tapestry,
A fragment in your galaxy,
A comma in your biography.
Just a pixel in your memory.

But a minute:
...A minute's long enough to think,
To fathom out your missing link.
A minute's short enough to dream,
To imagine that you've won and scream.

Intensive concentration meets
A thousand revs, a hundred beats,
An old familiar entity,
Big Apple time, expansively.
In extra time it feels like more,
Depending of course upon the score.

An hour
Is composed enough,
To organize time or attempt as much.
Because hours have a tendency
To compress, accelerate …then flee.

No, hours don't hang around too long.
The more you squeeze in,
The sooner they're gone.
So multi-taskers feel aggrieved

cont.

That whole mornings pass
With nout achieved.

A day,
That's all for our planet to rotate,
One dreamy daze,
One sleepless night,

A day is two relentless tides:
Commute / collapse,
Rest-up / revive.

A somersault of circumstance,
With tables turned,
A change of stance.

A week
Flies by like a quickening breeze,
Keeps naughty days in line with ease.
Keeps the wheels of business turning,
Keeps children smart and teachers learning.

A month,
A cycle,
A lunar phase.

Anticipated optimistically,
  Driven uncontrollably,
    Colliding unavoidably,
      Remembered sentimentally.

Enough to put you in arrears,
It's not as long as it appears.
Here's a heads-up: With heads kept down,
A month can force your smile to frown.

But a year
...Now there's some serious chunk of time!
When judges sentence, when terms define.

cont.

Just one lap around our sun
Gives oak its rings, prompts migration.
Or a landmark consigned to history.
Another birthday or anniversary.

Irresistible, it conquers fear,
To unchartered pages by pioneers
Who stand or fall by guile and luck,
They plan ahead they dive and duck.

...For you and I, best not try to shape it,
A year is precious.
Accept, embrace it.
Don't hesitate when it invites you in,
Proceed with cautious optimism.

A New Year ...the gateway of a maze,
Seconds, minutes, hours and days,
Weeks and months lie in wait,
Design their course and plot our fate.

So be warned, the New Year won't slow down for us,
Strap yourself in ...for breathlessness.
You could squander the year trying to shape it
Don't prevaricate,
Try not to waste it.

The annual chance to perfect (or improve at least),
To stay on course, to slay the beast.
To influence our history,
...At least 'til the end of January!

Where Is Love

When the council flats were failed by smoke alarms,
Our love was not enough.
When local authorities claimed their homeless were just fraudsters,
Our love was not enough.
When ministers choked the NHS,
Our love was not enough.
And when coal prices were more valued than the miners themselves,
Love was sadly, not enough.

But hold on,
When we watched, *It's a Wonderful Life*,
Surely love was quite enough.
And after that terrifying near miss I had,
Then love was all there was.
Yes, and free-falling into your bride's beaming eyes,
And again, holding the new-born ...what a moment,
Then love was more than enough.

So where did the message fade?
At what point was the miracle betrayed?
What's so strong as to twist the narrative out of recognition?
...Or rather, what's so weak as to allow it all to happen?
What corrodes and what corrupts?
What could pervert this pure perfection?

When sufficient is insufficient,
When excess becomes the norm.
When pride meets vanity,
And together they murder modesty.
And when humility has to accept that modesty's life is gone,
It backs away. It's overpowered.
Then greed, gorgeous greed,
Becomes the pilot and the steward.

With gorgeous greed in control, it's so much more straightforward.
Sympathy, empathy, tolerance ...gone.
So pull onto the hard shoulderless, super-highway of satisfaction
A truth, now without conscience,
A new reality of attraction.
Look at the new, liberated me,
In the Maserati of me,

                                                                                              cont.

Dressed in the labels of me,
For the indulgence of me.

But there's blood on the hands of gorgeous greed,
His prints on the crime scene for all to see,
So guilt and deception enter the stage,
With partners, pride and envy with wrath and lust and rage.
Powerful combinations, deadly gangsters of the soul,
The final occupation of the heart,
As sloth and gluttony take control.

They dress up desire and parade it on a leash,
As love substitute, love lite,
Prosecco love, Mercedes love,
Super Dry love, exclusive love,
Sinister love, conditional love.
Manipulative, deceptive, coercive love.
Like a toy dog in a handbag,
Ownership, gratification, vanity and control,
But for gorgeous greed and company,
They're as dissatisfied as before.

Now the gangsters use desire as a fashionable form of currency,
With which gorgeous greed creates transactions,
To produce false feelings of dependency,
So that all parties feel denied,
And the players feel deprived.
Yet in the struggle to conform - they still can't quite forget,
Like they're desperately vaping on a prosthetic cigarette.

So what is there for real love to do...?

Does it plan its revenge?
Does it fight its way back?
Does it wait for an opportunity?
Does it devise its attack?

...No, it doesn't even take sides.

Love's bravery is its consistency,
Its strength is its tenderness.
It doesn't seek supremacy,
Its pursuit is merely peacefulness.

cont.

Like a dandelion seed blown along a hillside,
The patient purpose, the jewel, the essence.
This love is the challenge,
The mystery, the test.
Elusive to gorgeous greed,
But in abundance to the meek.
Not just the solitary songbird,
But a murmuration of emotion,
An over-whelming concentration.
Not the soloist that infatuates,
But a choir. A choir of all who've loved and gone before.

Unobvious, but no less ubiquitous,
Love is under your nose.
Not just in the ambulances and on the wards,
But in Asda, amongst the hoards.
Not just at funerals and there amid the wedding,
But on the roads on which you drive,

See it,
Feel it,
Breathe it,
Inhale it.
Wear it like a badge, accept it as a tide,
Carry it like a banner with confidence and pride.

Find it,
Trust it,
Give it,
Take it.
Let it be the substance of every piece and every part,
Recognise those gangsters; perform a detox of the heart.
Because ...and my friend, you already have the proof.
Love's the most precious thing you'll ever find.

And that's the sacred truth.

Poor Little Rich Kid

The Poor Little Rich Kid was bored with his toys,
With his plasma TV and nights out with the boys.
Tired of his security and riches galore,
Privileges lost their lustre, he wanted much more.

The Poor Little Rich Kid's free thinking curtailed,
His intake of news reduced to reading The Mail.
So resentment soon flourished and bitterness reigned,
Warped nostalgia matured, fake independence regained.

But the Poor Little Rich Kid's frustrations grew stronger,
With Barnier and Davies's talks growing longer.
And those warnings of confidence and investment so fickle,
Former rivers of growth had reduced to a trickle.

Now the Poor Little Rich Kid blames it all on …whatever!
Negative campaigning, the media, the wife and the weather.
And whilst his naivety and arrogance, he privately regrets,
That Poor Little Rich Kid deserves all that he gets.

Rob Kersley

Wintry Lower Chapel with Corn Du in the distance

It's Only a House

Dismantling your home,
Packing away your life.
Stripping the creation
Off canvas, with knife.

Like a cardiac surgeon,
Bold incisions where we dwelled.
A heartectomy by bubble-wrap,
Transplanting the life that it held.

An urge to move on,
This instinctive upheaval.
As an act of ecdysis,
Shedding skin, for renewal.

Unpleasant,
Unsettling,
Unthinkable, somehow.

But,
Keeping the faith,
In a haven unknown.
Take a final, deep breath,
And reassurance of our own.
Then dive down through the wave,
Hand in hand.
Swim the cave,
Know that you'll break,
The surface somewhere,
To emerge,
To gasp, to breathe,
The cool air.

Going forward,
Together.
Believing,
As ever.
Our home now in boxes,
Our hearts in our mouths.
We're closing a door,
...Now it's only a house.

Rob Kersley

Before and After

After tired boots are unlaced,
After aching wrists are un-taped.
Before the dinners, black ties and a la carte subscriptions,
Before the bruises emerge and the lactate constrictions.

After the sayers have said and the doers have done,
After all those concerned, have accepted who won.
After the hype and after the show,
After the anthems, but before the last blow.

Before Italian fans turned up in blue wigs,
Before textured footballs succeeded the bladders of pigs.
Before kicking tees replaced pint glasses of sand,
Before we knew we had hamstrings, and we just ran on command.

Before there was sport there was untamed aggression,
Before our respect, they undermined to submission.
Before there was humility there were superior tones,
And before there was sportsmanship, there was ...Eddie Jones.

Rob Kersley

Elle Climber

At the approach, the long trek in,
The focus was endurance,
Playing the long game.
Navigating the sinkholes,
Critical selection of Sherpas,
Decisive dismissal of shirkers.

In those featureless days and nights,
Only she saw her potential.
Only she understood her objective.
And as the last of her couriers fell away,
As she emerged into the limelight from that endless jungle, alone,
As she contemplated that monstrous sheer rock face up close,
Only she had ever believed it to have been her destiny.

She accepted the challenge, though she would often question her motives.
She stepped over the remains of her predecessors,
Light-headed on success,
Blinded by an ambition,
Hijacked by her struggle,
Her ascent by attrition.

To that initial tentative, trembling, toe-hold,
The first fumbling, finger-tip fixture.
"*Short-term objectives*", her mantra: A ledge, a false-summit.
"*Medium-term Direction*", reading the featureless, sheerness, peerless vertical path.
Shallow breathing through pursed lips,
Cheek brushing the clammy rock face she grips.
Reminding herself of the view from below,
The view everyone else has,
The view she held onto, in those years of anonymity,
The view she now recalls, that she clutches like a Bible,
If not for real progress, then for her sheer survival.

Another layer of cloud.
Upwards into increasingly dizzying altitude.
Safety-ropes gambled and lost,
Escape routes long since passed
Crumbling ledges giving way under her feet,
Holding on with chalked fingerprints through determined, gritted teeth.

cont.

With the world looking on,
A catastrophic slip now overdue.
She no longer feels fear,
That died long ago.
That died when reality gripped her,
Like a virus she had denied.
That this pinnacle is no chalice,
That it's just another cog of the same treadmill.
The same story,
With the same ending.

Heroic failure will now be a relief.
As she looks down through the mist,
She picks her spot,
Prepares to fall.

A strong gust.
Another shower of hail,
But this one builds.
Darker clouds now,
Clinging to that tower.
Deepening, torrential, blinding, screaming winds,
A merciless gale,
A hurricane of events.

Exposure,
As only she and her kind experience,
When maternity got confused with servility.
...And push came to shove, came to pay gap, came to grope.
A self-sacrificial pursuit,
To fly the flag that she crocheted while others slept.
Defying the prejudice that possessed her.
Denying the established order of things.
Ascending, just to prove she could,
Climbing as she alone believed she would.
Her deliberate, formal assertion,
Born of decades of casual put-downs,
The product of countless demeaning one liners
By those cowardly, cynically, casual under-miners.

Icy numbness:
Rigid cyanosis.
Then tragically, inevitably,
The wet chalk slips in silence.
As she does.

Abstinence

Give it up for good, perhaps.
Cut the coaxial cord.
Unplug that wretched Wi-Fi,
Isolation then restored.

What difference could it make to me?
At least I'd rediscover sleep,
Insulated in my duvet,
A peaceful dreaming heap.

Wouldn't have to bury it deep,
Wouldn't have to find new hiding places every night.
Wouldn't wake at two am.
Demons evasive in the absence of light.
My subconscious having exhumed them yet again,
Left them prowling out of sight.

This inkling, this instinct,
That something bad is happening to those vulnerable millions.
The lure of knowledge,
The need to know the victims and the villains.

"Give it up for lent perhaps?"
I laughed ...she didn't.
"Seriously?" I said. "No news, like those wise monkeys."
She laughed ...I didn't.

But I did it...
A current affairs cold-turkey.
An abstinence of blow by blow doom predictions,
Like a Dyno-Rod, colonic,
A pause in the commentary of dereliction.

But Lent finished yesterday,
Forty days and forty nights.
I missed it all initially,
But when the withdrawal symptoms eased
The peace returned that only sleep can bring.
Refreshing like a breeze.

cont.

But Lent finished yesterday,
So I missed the forecasters' crow
And I didn't see the weather warnings,
So how was I to know,
Blissfully, peacefully unaware,
Of, *yet more heavy snow*.

It had indeed snowed overnight,
But by seven it had turned to rain.
Piles of snow had slid off our car,
But rain dissolved it yet again.
The *severe disruptions* that I didn't hear,
Didn't happen.
The *travel chaos* headlines that I missed,
Didn't occur.
I slept through the illuminations,
The rolling news,
The thirty minute updates,
The stream of gloom
The doom predictions, the premonitions, the news productions.
The Pandora's Box,
Of perplexing, panoramas of paranoia,
Our LCD Panasonic producing practically perfect images,
Of partially possible possibilities,
But penetrating, permeating and pre-disposing
My very persona with what amounts to poisonous pollution.
The endless feed of information that I thought I had to know,
And by morning I was unaware,
That equilibrium had somehow been restored.

Yes, I arose bleary-eyed this morning,
Having slept like a log as they say,
And, with Lent a safe distance behind me,
Read the dog-eared headlines of yesterday.

But thankfully, the world hadn't ended,
The Easter sun had risen again.
The near miss had happened without me
And life, thank God goes on.

Escape

I take myself away sometimes,
When I can no longer stand the news.
Follow the path, up over the hills,
To inhale, to digest the views.

I climb until I'm gazing down,
On the miniature, model-sized objects.
The silent perspective simplifies.
Thoughts carried up, slide out of context.

I take myself away sometimes,
When I can't believe those comments.
Down by the bridge, I watch the river,
Lost in reflection, carried away on the currents.

Fresh water by the seamless mile,
Continuity of gravity ...of energy,
Circulation, evaporation, irrigation.
Not new but recycled, endlessly.

I take myself away sometimes,
When their selfishness suffocates.
I can be there, down in Cot Valley again,
And let the heaving power resuscitate.

The fullness of the ocean from the edge of land.
Hugging my knees, watching the spray at dawn.
Doing what it's been doing since we first had the sun and the moon,
What it'll be doing for millennia after we're gone.

I can take my mind away at any time,
When perspective's been misplaced.
When I need reminding that I began as a miracle,
A one in a million chance.

There has to be more to us than carbon,
I don't care that there's no proof.
More than just this fragile flesh,
And these bodies which cause such strife.

When the setting is the timelessness around us,
And our frailties are exposed once more,
When the backcloth bears the teachings

cont.

Rob Kersley

Of all who have gone before.

When I've been away sometimes,
I remember that my tenure is fleeting at best.
That everything ever gained will be lost,
And that the soul is the one ...the only thing,
In which I should invest.

St Donald & St Nigel

How can I ever repay the debt,
For my superego's revival.
Unshackled from my liberal conscience,
Saint Donald and Saint Nigel.

In those dark days of my ignorance,
When I believed my failures to be my own.
You gave me someone else to blame,
Saint Donald and Saint Nigel.

Yes, come to think of it you're right,
That language always resonated in my mind.
And the permission you gave to say it out loud has made obscenities cool again,
Saint Donald and Saint Nigel.

And your prophesy continues,
For now that my hatred's freely spoken,
It turns out that they loathe me too, just like you always said they did.
Saint Donald and Saint Nigel.

This isolation feels so natural,
No synagogues, mosques or temples.
Keep those scapegoats off this wised-up island ...Britannia, land of purity!
Saint Donald and Saint Nigel.

Yes, I agree. It's them against us. And yes, this was (I suppose) always the case.
So when war becomes unavoidable then ok, my great grand-children will pay the price of my ignorance.
For U-turns will be impossible by then,
Saint Donald and Saint Nigel.

Rob Kersley

The Tragic Garthbrengy Murder

Anser, my middle-aged neighbour,
Guarded his timber-framed home with his life.
Unreasonably, aggressive to me,
Mostly when he was around his wife.

Like a strutting, stern Centurion,
Patrolling the perimeter of his plot.
Any approach was met with an outburst,
Of expletives that he frequently spat.

But something about his dignity,
And in the passion that he held,
That in spite of his need for anger management,
I was intrigued and somehow compelled.

Then, on that Friday in mid-April,
Anser's world suddenly fell apart.
He didn't try to contain his cries,
Days, weeks, months. His lost love, broke his heart.

The murder scene; under the chestnut tree,
Though Anser wasn't allowed near.
No murder weapon in evidence,
And no apparent motive was clear.

Anser's purpose had been stripped from him,
She was his world, as he was hers once.
And time wasn't the great healer,
But a space to find acceptance.

Meanwhile, the hardest winter in over thirty years.
Sub-zero for months and months on end.
And for Vulpes, a single struggling mother of three,
It was a lonely survival without a single friend.

She'd suspected, she wasn't much good at anything,
She thought that it explained why it had always felt so tough.
So she fed her children before her withering self,
But for her starving kids there was never nearly enough.

cont.

As Christmas froze to January, her cheeks hollowed.
And in February's half-light, her senses were dimming.
By early April, she was blinded by her hunger,
Drowning in starvation her blurred vision was now swimming.

Her once glossy red hair was now coming out in clumps,
Despairing Vulpes, at her wits' end, had to take action.
Reckless if she did, but suicide if she didn't.
So as the ground moved beneath her, she somehow found traction.
Exhausted, but she's done it. Bloodied, she now returns home,
And the family have food again; it's been such a long time.
But in her blissfully deep, contented, guilty sleep,
She twitches herself awake as she re-enacts her crime.

Anser Domesticus tucks his head under his wing,
He still sees her blood-stained white feathers, his anguish, his strife.
The vixen's murder scene, the sombre shade of that tree,
Where Vulpes Vulpes did what she did, and took his beloved wife.

Russia 2018

"He's the new Messi". The commentator waxed lyrical,
Just before he fell, his agony clearly visible.
But the action replay made his contortions somewhat questionable,
His English teammates surround the ref, all pretty hysterical.
"How's my hair?" He sobs to the pitch side hairdresser,
"Can you fix it again?" Glancing back to the aggressor.
"Are you ok now, Sweet Prince?" Asks the mullet assessor,
He limps back up the pitch to confront the transgressor.

"He has genius pace!" The TV presenter gushed.
Just before the collision, in which he appeared to be crushed.
But the action replay made his stagecraft unjust,
His French teammates surround the ref who appears nonplussed.
"Comment estmeschevaux?" He asks his *salon de coiffure*,
"Tresserioux!" He says. "Vousavez le sideburn rupture!"
"Merde!" Screams the Sweet Prince. "Le diabolique provocateur!"
He hobbles back up the pitch to *affronte le oppresseur*.

"There was definitely contact." Noted the match analyst.
When it seemed that some consciousness had ceased to exist.
But the action replay had his feigning dismissed,
His Mexican teammates mob the ref, retreating in their midst.
"Como es mi cobello?" He asks his *peluquero de emergencia*,
"Es un disaster!" He says. "Ustedtienne un dislocado de la fringe!"
"Maravilloso!" Shrieks the Sweet Prince. "El miserable monstruo!"
He staggers up the wing to confront *suagresor*.

From scissor kicks and critics,
To theatrics and histrionics.
Paediatric melodramatics,
Then obstetric biometrics.
Dirty tricks and analgesics,
And psychiatric economics.
I know the World Cup's meant to unify,
But I get turned off when they glorify.
And the reason ...I'm not gonna lie,
Is 'cos poor Wales failed to qualify!

Rob Kersley

Cornish Reflection

We walked from turquoise Porthcurno,
Side by side, hip by hip
In the warm, lavender breeze,
Then sat and watched the swallows dance.
We stood above the towering silent cliffs
And the solemn, surging swell.
Captivated in an eternal,
Tireless, timeless trance.

We watched in silent awe,
At the Brison's crimson sunset.
The ball of fire dripping its molten dew,
Across sea and land.
Its life fading,
Sinking from sight in all finality.
As I was, before you reached out,
And took my trembling hand.

Rob Kersley

The River and the Rock

(For the occasion of my wonderful father's 90th birthday, I wanted to write about how it feels for me to be one of four active and individual siblings who have *our Dad* as our dad.)

The path from the hill to the shoreline,
The journey from source to sea.
The flow of the river, the carriageway,
Of our lives relentlessly.
But looping, rhythmic currents emerge,
Elongated swirls around deep pools.
So the river flows upstream sometimes,
As the gravitational touchstone pulls.

From the gurgling brook of an infant,
I was a stream of bright surprise.
Bubbling, babbling to show you my treasures,
Maple leaves and dragon flies.
So many vivid images,
All seasons intertwined.
Downstream to youth, the race was on,
You were watching from behind.

To the torrent of adolescence,
In spate and then in drought,
I ebbed and flowed, I rose and fell,
But never was in doubt,
Of the immoveable feature that watched over me,
In the certainty of love.
You created an eddy that guided me,
From below and from above.

And now as I continue my journey,
Past the bridges and the bends.
The sparkling, bright reflections,
Of my own life as it wends.
I'm seeing your influence once more,
In my purpose and my shape.
From your steadfast, magnetic permanence,
I hope never to escape.

cont.

Rob Kersley

An antidote to ostentation,
To vanity and greed.
Unshakable in your devotion,
With a family to feed.
And thirty-two thousand suns later,
And over a thousand new moons old,
Your quiet truth surrounds you,
What a legacy to behold.

Such steadfast strength,
What an awesome, tender force.
To resist my changing currents,
To influence my course.
And now the morning mist of my youth has cleared,
For me to reflectively take stock:
I recognize you my father,
In our river, you're the rock.

Don't Go Near the News Today

If Trump's got your fingers in your ears,
If Putin's put you behind the sofa again.
If May has made you beg for Prozac,
Then you really shouldn't go near the news today.

Do they know what they're doing to us?
Is our cowering reaction what they actually seek?
Brandishing loaded Kalashnikovs,
Controlling by fear and making us meek.

If you're done with screaming at the TV,
Peering through the cracks between your fingers,
You'd think that they'd invented *doublethink*.
No, don't go near their toxic news today.

Can you believe her hypocrisy?
Bombing, as *humanitarian aid*!
That's just what those poor souls need right now,
A massive escalation in the stakes.

See it all for what it is my friend,
See us for what we are and all the others too.
Scrutinize your thoughts ruthlessly
And see yourself anew.

Dig, until you find your fear,
Then…
Cut it away if it offends thee,
For fear is imagined,
Pluck it and cast it from thee.
For fear is contagious,
And yearns to be fed.

All life is truly sacred,
And it's yours and mine to lose.
So please, promise me this one thing,
That today, you won't watch the news.

HEALTH   DEAR DEIDRE   TECH   TRAVEL   MOTORS   PUZZLES   SUN BINGO

COMMENT

News > Opinion

LETTERS SPECIAL Sun readers say Boris Johnson is bang on about the burka — and attacks on the British way of life need to stop

'Boris must also be allowed to speak honestly, he has nothing to apologise for'

The Sun
1:01 14 Aug 2018   Updated 2:44 14 Aug 2018

Sketch by Rob Kersley 2022

Hate Criminal

It was delivered on the pavement
Near the park,
By a terrier
Whose owner didn't care.
It sat there abandoned,
Steaming of *Its* own accord,
Self-conscious, embarrassed, naked, laid bare.

It saw her approaching,
In her new white trainers
Round the corner she ran,
Late.
Pigtails flailing,
Homework in bag.
If only *It* could have called out,
To try to make *It*self heard,
Before the inevitable
Disastrous squishing occurred.

Not for *Its* own sake,
But for hers in her trainers so chaste.
In *It*self, inert, intact,
Primed and laced.
But with no voice, no chance
And feeling debased,
It sat and awaited *Its* sticky fate,
Full of regret, such is waste.

Others have choice,
Others have a chance.
Others have a voice
To express and enhance.
But others, some others
Choose offence.
Yes others, some others
Use offence.

Some use that voice,
To attack women.
Islamic women

cont.

Whose culture requires
A certain dress-code,
A modesty, a constraint.
But it makes them easy to pick out,
To target, to discriminate.

The lads will grow
To love him,
Eccentric Brit.
Shoots from the hip
From a safe distance.
For his is a world away,
From streets where hard earned ethnic harmony abides.
Where evermore casual racism (his favourite kind),
Will belittle all sides.

Back to the pavement,
Moments before impact.
Minutes before
Her new white trainers
Would be contaminated.
A full hour before, no matter how
She scraped and scuffed
And scuffed and scraped
They would never feel the same again.

Those moments before
She would step on *It*,
The anxiety *It* felt, the self-loathing,
If *It* could be anything else ...but not this.
It sat there sweating, thinking of *its* impact on the innocent.
While others, with a lesser moral code than *It*
Do not.

The difference then:
An accidental incident
To a motivated stimulant.
Harmony so precious, so fragile
Easily unpicked
By agitators, so vile.
No accident this insult,

                                                            cont.

And no sincere apology
Will therefore result.

A dangerous man
In sheep's clothing,
Monitoring a global surge
To the right.
Calculating his support for all he's worth.
Hurling boulders of reckless language.
Creating reactionary waves on which to surf.
Populist,
Blatant hate crimes.
...A dangerous man, in dangerous times.

Rob Kersley

Venus

To the chancel of an Irish King's daughter,
In Bri's Beetle, Venus arrived.
We tied our knot where Saint Buriana lay
As the universe had contrived.

Our sun appeared just as the weatherman said,
Its second nearest planet flared.
While *my* Venus stepped into that sacred place,
With flowers platted in her hair.

Reciprocated, blindfolded leaps of faith,
At the altar, in a bubble,
This gift, that promise "we'll never look back".
Like a Phoenix from the rubble.

I never see them when they first enter in,
'Til they land on my toast or knee.
Or sat there on the rim of my flippin' cup
Or doing breaststroke in my tea!

But Venus leaps, table to sofa to chair,
Like D'Artagnan with her swatter.
Swish, Thwack, Slap, With panache and zeal..."Got him, Ha!
…That horrible little rotter!"

Humming, I put the kettle on, by the sink,
When Venus bounds like a gazelle.
Woody observes, looking bored. He knows the score,
Venus five, "Two injured aswell!"

A Munster Chief's daughter, Saint Buriana.
In whose shrine we commenced our life.
Me and my true goddess of love and beauty,
And intrepid trapper of flies!

The Chocoholic

I heard that alluring voice cry out,
At twenty minutes to tea.
"Just a single square", it clearly said.
"I'm exactly what you need".

It crept in again at seven o'clock,
"Your energy levels are low.
Two little squares should do the trick,
To fill that square-sized hole".

It called out once more at ten past eight,
"It's release those endorphins time!
Three chunky squares this time then,
'Cos endorphin constraints a crime".

Once more it nagged at quarter to ten,
"I think we both know what you need,
Four lovely squares can't do any harm,
You'd hardly call that greed".

"You can't leave those five squares over-night",
It whispered at ten twenty-eight.
"Best to finish them off and have done with it,
Diet tomorrow with a good clean slate".

So they checked me into cocoa rehab.
"You've got it bad", said the suit and the nurse.
"Two kilos a day is pretty hard-core,
And at ninety per cent, it doesn't get much worse".

They led me through to my de-tox prep,
Body cavity search ...nightmare!
And claimed they found a Cadbury's Creme Egg!
I've no idea how that got there.

Thirty days on a diet of bran
This pure white cell became home.
They said, "chew on this carob if things get too much",
A sort of cocoa methadone.

cont.

I've been clean now for thirty-two weeks,
"*Each day's a victory*", did the trick.
That, and the photo for emergency use,
Of Donald Trump eating a Twix.

So I speak now as a reformed chocoholic,
Having kicked the wicked bean.
Cocoa psychedelia is a one way street,
So nibble responsibly, please!

Long in the Tooth

"These shadows are the roots, here and here".
Mariana, my young but sincere
And long suffering Spanish dentist
Traces my x-rays like an artist.
"Now, I can drill out the root canals,
And remove the nerves from where they lurk,
But there's no guarantee this will work."

"Why not?" I ask most respectfully.
Mariana says, "Well here you see…"
Drumming the x-rays like a castanet
"Is the bone, and the root which I suspect
Now above your gum line ...such retraction!
So we may be looking at extraction".

"Oh no", I say to my dental youth.
"What then, don't say I'll have a false tooth?"
"If you so wish", says she.
"Or an implant maybe".

Side-saddle, straddling. I'm thinking *strewth!*
Gulping, disbelieving, *"A false tooth!"*.
A false tooth! … "False teeth!" ...could it really be?
Feels like only last week, I turned thirty!
"False teeth!" Too young, too soon. Not yet.
"False teeth!" Too warm, mouth dry, palms wet.

"We will also need to discuss these."
Mariana's holding a mirror
For me to see my odd-looking teeth.
Are those really mine? ...Like tired rows
Of derelict white marble headstones,
Or scrapped white cars with mercury grey
Body panels. Misshapen. Imbedded
With amalgam, my cavities
Could be creating world scarcities!

Odd shaped teeth, all with fillings ...unnatural.
Some look like chewed up Mint Imperials,
Others, broken Polos pressed into

                                                               cont.

Gums of Foam Shrimps. Quite a few like Love Hearts,
At least one Fizzer and a couple
Of Parma Violets. I can't estimate
How they came to be in such a state.

They say ageing's a natural thing,
Doesn't feel too natural to me.
I was quite happy as I was, back
When my hair was still so youthfully black,
And I didn't spend the first few
Minutes of every waking day
Talking about my last night's sleep.

Stranger still would be a Benjamin
Buttonesque existence, of reverse
Ageing. Or, held in suspension
While the others followed convention.

So here we all are:
Making our way up the same steep hill,
Carrying our personalized
Invisible baggage, under arms,
On our shoulders, in our hearts, in heads.
Passing the same land marks. Resting where
We need. Stopping for a while at increments
That later, will become significant.

So Mariana has been chosen to
Bring me this thickly accented message:
"Your gums ...they recede you know? But eet's ok.
Eet's just a tiny ting that happens."
Her Catalan smile delivers the harsh report
Softened in Barcelona warmth.

Receding blimmin' gums,
Getting longer in the tooth!
A searing nudge, this toothache.
Making me stop.
Reminding me where I am.
Forcing me to focus
On my location,

cont.

Looking back down
The winding path
That carried me here,
Then peering upwards through the mist,
To plot the course I believe exists.

...And no,
It's not because I've just found my glasses in the fridge again,
Or that I'm staring down the barrel of my first denture.
After all, I've still got a few of my marbles left,
And I can still fart with confidence!

Objectives will prove irrelevant,
At a summit, ever diminishing.
The climb: Both the price and the prize.
Closing my eyes.
The journey is the gift,
My dentist leans over
...And the drilling begins.

When Kipling Discovered Curry

If you can keep your poppadums when all about you
Are losing theirs and blaming it once again on you,
Or keep talking when the waiters can't understand you,
But make patient allowances for their doubting too;
If you can chew and not be tired-out by the chewing,
Or being lied about, don't deal in Indian pork pies,
Or being battered, don't give way to their battering,
And yet don't chat with boiled rice, nor talk to Indian fries:

If you search for karma- and not make korma your master;
If you seek to josh- and not make rogan josh your aim;
If you can meet with Tesco Tinned Tikka and chicken Vesta
And treat those two mass-produced impostors just the same;
If you can bear to see the things you earlier dropped
Blended with turmeric to make beef biryani.
Or watch the things you ordered, now dripping down your top,
Then stoop, sway and clean 'em up with a worn out chapati:

If you can make a heap of your prawn crackers and all
And risk it on one turn of "onion bhaji - or- bust",
And lose, and then are down to your very last cheese ball
And never breathe a word about your very public loss;
If you can force your heart and thought and nerve and sinew
To keep on eating so long after your friends are gone,
And later, hold on when the loo's not where you left it
And have the determined will which says to you: "Hold on!"

If you can talk to crowds and keep your food inside you,
Or walk to The Castle- and not lose the common touch,
If neither lambkeema nor vindaloo can hurt you,
If you like it hot and it's never, ever too much;
If you can always fill the unforgiving minutes
With sixty-odd sizzling seconds' worth of beef madras,
Yours is Brecon's Zeera and everything that's in it,
And- which is very much more- you'll be a Naan my son!

Rob Kersley

Rosa Hubermann

Sometime between her SATs
And her A-levels,
After My Little Pony
And before her first car
An event took her.
Made its mark, left her branded,
Deeply scarred.

And whatever that was
Would overshadow the success
Whatever occurred
Would play on constant repeat,
On a screen behind reality.
Invading her dreams
To become the platform, the canvas
For all she would achieve.
Blistering the perfect
Acrylic landscape,
Never more than a light scratch
From the surface.

So she developed
A coping mechanism.
Where she sought events,
That made hers not uncommon.

She pursued anguish,
Clung to the difficulty,
The tragedy, the sadness,
To normalise her scars.

Only in misery, did she find comfort,
Torture became her shelter.
Captive in an unlocked cell,
Trapped in tribulation.
Wrapped in wretchedness,
Increasingly dependent,
Then clinging, reliant,
Engaged then wed.
Uncanny,

cont.

Rob Kersley

A Stockholm Syndrome of the spirit.

A kinder heart you'll seldom find.
Such soul and honour,
Benevolence and charity.
But on edge around merriment,
Malcontent,
Cherophobic, joy averse.
And yet for Liesel,
The foster child she would come to secretly adore,
Tenderness was hidden behind *saumensch!*
Love buried beneath *saukerl!*

She doesn't want your cheer
And your sympathy will be thrown to the floor.
Like the Mandarin soldiers or ducks in a row,
Well drilled,
Practised.
Woes memorized, rehearsed by rote.

And the longer she avoided
Going toe to toe with her demons
The less she mourned the imprisonment of *das kind*.
So when the droplets that once dropped
From her porcelain features stopped,
She would never leave her captor
And step out into the sun.

Don't Stare Into the Sun

Don't stare into the sun,
Nor claw at the ground.
Searching for answers,
Not ready to be found.

The burning
Eternity,
Of a churning
Agony,
Will leave us
Asking why.
But light and life
And warmth and love,
With time
Will pacify.

Closed eyes in solemn acceptance,
Of where all beginnings begun.
Your search could leave you blind
My love.
...Don't stare into the sun.

Rob Kersley

James Gatz

His placid home
Where truth was unthreatened.
With no hunger for appetite,
And no appetite for hunger.

Where endless prairies
Were measured by stoic labour.
Where enough would suffice
And harmony was the fabric
Richly embossed
With contentment.

Then ambition settled
On this farmer's boy,
From serene North Dakota.
Like pollen floating,
In an indigo night sky.
Inhaled,
Agitating innocent airways.
Germinating discontent
In his deepest of sleeps.

Young James Gatz,
Newly blighted by vexation.
Waking from his American Dream,
Resentful.

A desire igniting his ideality,
But sidelined from opportunity.
Frustrated,
Angry,
Tension builds.

Then, a discovery.
Alchemy ...no less.
Something from nothing,
A trick, a short-cut.
Just a callow embellishment ...almost fact.
Then exaggeration ...playfully romanticized.
Unchallenged falsehoods,
Naively trusted.
Half-truths become whole lies.

cont.

Lines crossed,
Trusts betrayed.

To the rebirth…
The re-inventor
Who fell down from the sky,
Reborn in East Egg,
A short swagger from Manhattan.
With a brand new past,
From pristine metamorphosis.
Where lies became his new craft.
New life,
New home,
New name…
Where Jay Gatsby would flourish.
Where Jay Gatsby would devour.

When sufficient pressure builds.
When greed and envy swell,
To split open a soul that spills
Words of least resistance tell
For acts to follow later
With scruples relegated to that,
Of a mere guilty spectator.

But somewhere deep within his soul,
There still beat a conscience.
Worn down …cowering
Under a furnace of desire.

It still pricks him,
Albeit flinching, timid, scorched.
Telling him that his lies
Whilst a perfect alibi,
Are a base crime,
A prime sin.
The easiest way out
To say it never happened,
To claim it was never said.
And each untruth picks away at the threads,
The tapestry of trust.
Every deception pulls at the loose ends
Of the webbing of communities.

                                                            cont.

Every fabrication turns us into islands.
Untrusted, untrusting.
Sceptical, suspicious.
Envious, embittered.
Intolerant and vicious.

Sat amidst the most treacherous tangle of webs,
His final desire.
A revelation of honesty,
Of love.
A heart still true
In a life of complete distortion.
Unmistakable in a hall of mirrors.
When despite an empire of fiction,
Daisy nearly succumbed
To the dazzling bright lies,
Over the mundane truth.
And the liar …whom so nearly survived.

Rob Kersley

Amir

They knew their places,
Or thought they did.
Young boys, best friends,
From different ends
Of that same
Tranquil, Afghan garden.

He might have weighed in.
In that moment
That came without notice,
That went without closure.
He might have been cut and bruised,
But saved from a lifetime of torture.
If someone had warned him,
If someone had told him
That guilt can kill you.

Disgrace distilled over decades.
What price
Amir would pay in the end,
For redemption.
And how willingly
He would pay it.

Back he went into darkest Kabul,
With resolve and belief
Knotted gut, gritted teeth
Descending into a dog pit of damnation.
Years later, now as an adult,
On a mission of redemption.
Invaluable, his friend's son's life to rescue.
Incalculable, his tarnished soul to redeem.

That monster facing him again.
"A fight to the death for the Hazara".
The highest stakes,
The worst odds,
The greatest courage.
The most to win,
The least to lose.

cont.

Rob Kersley

Today he runs,
With young Sohrab.
Warm Californian wind in his hair,
The sun on his face.
Glowing in his heart.

That haunting pledge from Hassan,
The Kite Runner:
"For you a thousand times over",
He now promises,
In his liberation from shame.

So young, too soon
For that harshest test,
That he came to believe,
Defined him.
Unjust, unfair as life can be.
Thereafter became
The subplot to his story,
His life's work
To disprove.

His journey
Of self-atonement,
His quest for equilibrium.
Its purpose then,
Its reason ...to raise his game.
Inner peace at last,
Completeness.

Polskie Wroble

Small movements,
Sharp features.
Complex chirps,
Tender creatures.

To eat and sleep in their nest,
Surrounded
By precious images of fledglings flown,
On sideboards, on the walls
Of their perfect,
Well hidden home.

Spend one night under a Polish roof.
Feel the inaudible, high frequency hum
Of east European tension.
Those post-soviet times,
Too harsh,
Too strained to mention.

But you see it
When they don't hold your gaze,
Not so very distant,
Those heavy, iron days.

And yet this Polskie generosity…
In spite of the hand they've been dealt
It makes me sit my sorry self down,
To have a serious word
With my lucky, lucky self.

Polish sparrows,
Hard fought.
I caught
In their chattering
Heads cocked, a smattering
Of how comfortable
They know
That we've had it.

cont.

But, keeping their faith,
They kept their words.
Such big hearts
For such beautiful,
Little birds.

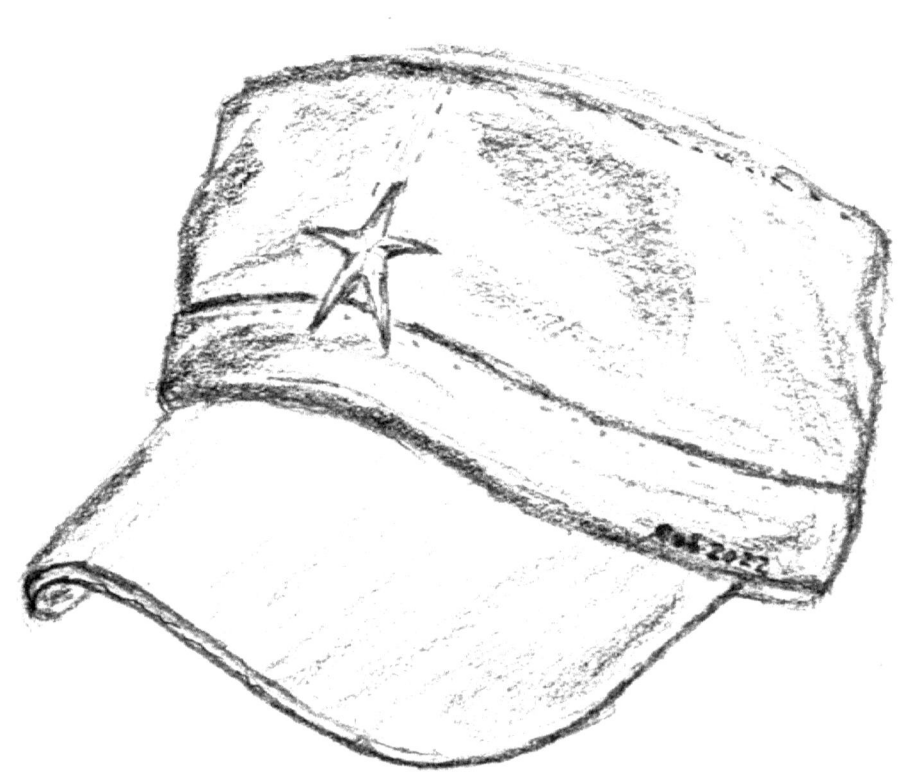

Comrade Corbyn

Comrade Corbyn emerges,
From his Comrade Corbyn nest.
In his Comrade Corbyn Castro cap
And Comrade Corbyn vest.

After months of hibernation,
Eyes adjusting to this dawn.
Unsteady, on his waking legs
And stifling a yawn.

Examining the berries,
Then scenting at the breeze.
He's timing his involvement,
He's jangling his keys.

They say he has Momentum,
That it's his destiny, his prize.
But I'm not sure he even wants office,
He just likes to theorize.

He's standing at the lectern,
Having something of a dig.
But his words are strange and clumsy
And his jacket's way too big.

Now Comrade Corbyn's centre stage
Yet still, it makes no sense.
That such an impact can be made,
Whilst sitting on the fence.

Yes, the polls all seem consistent,
But the thing I just don't get.
Is, how desperate must the others be,
If he's our safest bet.

Rob Kersley

Bishop Myriel

He appeared through the mist,
Which parted,
Like stage curtains concealing
A life of destitution.

He appeared through the mist,
Like a longboat approaching.
With grave purpose,
With gravitas.

Like a longboat approaching,
As a Viking funeral.
Ablaze. His defiant soul
Readied for its end.

Ablaze. His defiant soul,
To find an unsuspecting host,
Who did
The most unnatural thing.

To find an unsuspecting host:
Bishop Myriel, *"haunted by the ghost of social justice"*.
Disarmed the devil in Valjean,
With forgiveness.

Bishop Myriel, *"haunted by the ghost of social justice"*,
The greatest of men,
Starving hate of its food,
Starved that burning ship of oxygen.

The greatest of men,
Saw the broken soul
In his darkest hour,
And created a saint.

In his darkest hour,
To find forgiveness, such a rarity,
And a saint created:
Two, in fact.

London Calling

Shafts of hazy sunlight
Find gaps in the iconic towering sandstone,
Lighting the bright flags.
Determined truth, forcing itself into the streets of the capital.

Overhead; galleons of banners,
Union Jacks with circles of stars.
Carried by all classes,
Rolling with the masses.
From Benbecula to Brighton,
And Falkirk to Falmouth.

Leavers and Remainers,
On crutches and in trainers.
In wheelchairs, in prams,
Stride for stride, hand in hand.
Carpenters and Cleaners,
Students and their Teachers.
Seven hundred thousand, politely angered
By the Emperor's new clothes,
Having looked to their respective leaders,
Duplicity in that bright, low autumn light... exposed.

A common voice of unity,
Rejecting Farage's xenophobic vagary,
And his Brut-based Bond Moneypenny fantasies.
Opportunists, who took advantage of good people,
Like colonies to colonise,
Austerity beaten and brutalized
Through lies and lies and lies.

We should know there are no guarantees in
These shapeshifters with their degrees in
Politics, man it's treason!
Their last priority this mid-season,
Is protecting and serving and feeding
These seven hundred thousand voices of reason.
But second time around,
Our ignorance will be no defence.
And second time around
Their lies will be an indictable offence.

cont.

Rob Kersley

Mine was a single voice amid London calling,
And though I fear
Our cries will be denied.
I want to be able to tell my grandchildren,
That we were there.
We marched.
We tried.

I'll Be Home for Christmas Part 2

I wanted to write another piece to highlight the escalating homelessness problems in our country. I sat down and began the process by reading a poem I sent out last year. Unfortunately I then developed some tunnel vision and became slightly obsessed with the character again. Since, in the context of homelessness I could only think about the young woman in that original piece, I then decided to develop that original narrative rather than starting from scratch. Therefore, the following poem begins with the original, but the second part completes the story.

The warm glow from shop windows as I stroll back up The Hayes,
Crowded streets and crazy, jam-packed stores. It's that time of year again.
Busy plans, happy deadlines, merry chaos, joyous malls,
Gordon's, Riocha, Brains SA …and paracetamol.

A daze of contactless five card tricks, all running to chase the ace.
SAD condition and chronic winter blues have vanished without a trace.
Mentally ticking off my list, back on the heaving street,
I caught her eye, this foetal young woman. She wasn't shopped off her feet.

Curled up like a kitten on her cardboard bed with stained sleeping bag all about,
I was striding by with bags in hand, done in and all shopped out.
Back through the crowds, her stone grey face, I caught a glimpse once more,
Her vacant stare into vacant space, outside that vacant store.

I denied my selective conscience, just as far as Toys R Us,
Tried to convince myself it's her free choice, if she wants to sleep rough.
But by the time I reached the NCP, I was going back full tilt,
Was this compassion, morbid curiosity or was I driven by some kind of guilt?

I took her a cup of hot chocolate and a handful of paltry silver,
Her tearful gratitude humbled me, said she was too tired and hungry to shiver.
I asked how long she'd been lying there; she pulled her arm out from under her hip,
She glanced at a photo …then looked away, biting her trembling lip.

She shrugged and stuffed her arms into her armpits; she had dried blood around her mouth,
Said it all went wrong when her mum's new man moved in, and that's when she moved out.
She sniffed and said, *I can't go back, suicidal that would be,*
Then half-coughed, half-sobbed; *I can't believe, that this is happening to me.*

I asked about the photo in her hand. She said, *that's Mum and Dad and me,*
Dad was taken from us before his time. Hit and run near our house in Leigh.
I think me and Mum went into free-fall. I worry about her a lot.
This new guy she's got …complete psycho, I think she's lost the plot.

cont.

Rob Kersley

She looks again at the photo, *Dad's death was so unfair,*
As she speaks I see she's lost a tooth. I ask, what happened there?
Oh that, that's the psycho's handiwork, didn't like me saying 'no'.
He grabbed my arm but I got away, that's why I can't go home.

I've got to go, but don't go away. I didn't like leaving her on her own,
I march to a café and search for homeless charities on my phone.
I rang the number, and begged the gentle voice on the other end,
Can you help? She is so vulnerable; she has no family or friends.

We'll try, she said, *but it's Christmas ...you know. I'll see what we can do,*
It's getting worse though every year, not just adults, it's children too.
One hundred and twenty-eight thousand kids without a home this Christmas ...it's bleak.
And around a hundred and forty more families, becoming homeless every week.

What? How? I ask. Where's it going wrong?
Debt? Repossessions? ...The State can't cope, we've known this all along.
They live in hostels, B and B's, temporary accommodation awaited,
This end of the foodchain are the suffocated,
The relegated, the relocated and inevitably repudiated.

I ended the call more focused and determined to try to help.
I'll go to Cotswold's, buy her another sleeping bag, the warmest one they sell.
Then I wondered if I should. Is it appropriate, would it offend or not?
I'll ask her first. I left the café, and jogged back to her spot.

She was gone! No sight, no sign of her, just her soggy cardboard bed.
Which way? I darted up and down, my mind was full of dread.
She'd gone, disappeared. But what /who had taken her?
Despondent, I trudged back to the car, the last two hours seemed like a blur.

Driving back over the Beacons. Trance-like, preoccupied and so sad I could have cried.
In my climate controlled car, back to my family, back to my home.
Back to my centrally heated home ...imagine not having a home!
Back to my wife and my family ...imagine being totally alone!

I think of her missing tooth, her smile, dried blood under her nose.
I imagine one hundred and twenty-eight thousand children,
Abandoned, forsaken, dispossessed and still the number grows.
One hundred and forty more families each week, and that's in the UK alone,
I give thanks for the life I find myself in, but question the favouritism shown.

cont.

Dropping down from Storey Arms, I turn on the radio to change the context,
But they're playing, The Manics', *If You Tolerate This, Then your Children Will Be Next*.
I change channels and now it's Bing Crosby's, *I'll Be Home for Christmas*.
This has got to be coincidence? ...But even so, it's vicious.

Suddenly, I'm kicking off my shoes inside my familiar front door.
Solemnly, I'm walking up the stairs onto the kitchen floor.
Sullenly, I put the shopping down. I answer, Yes, I'm OK.
Actually no, I'm not. How could I be? ...nothing is OK!

I tell my family about that poor homeless girl from Leigh,
Then I tell them what the girl at the homeless charity told me:
That homelessness has doubled in the last seven years alone,
And in that time, our government has made 452 separate announcements,
...As if that will atone!
...But there's never any action,
The homeless don't have influence, so the homeless don't have traction.
So there's never any money,
Never for these people,
And there's never been so many,
And it's never felt so pitiful.

It's never been so one sided, so greedy and so wrong,
And it's never gonna change until we see beyond our own.
Because, '*Charity Begins at Home*' is a myth that undermines
The very meaning of the word that it was once meant to define!

They're all looking at me now and I know I'm making them stare,
But I still see her bloodied nose, her broken tooth and matted hair.

What does it say about you and I,
That we let them down this way?
And how will we justify ourselves to God on judgement day?

So we thought we'd have a turkey this year,
We thought we'd make mulled wine.
It dropped down to minus two last night,
But indoors, I'm feeling fine.
But the instinct of this season,
Remains as basic as it seems.
That's why she will be home for Christmas

cont.

Rob Kersley

...If only in her dreams.

That festive season went
With much less fanfare than when it came.
And my thoughts returned to appointments and plans
As those around me did the same.

The New Year's blank canvas
Urged me forward,
And winter thawed as it must.
And through the spring and dry, warm summer
My festive beacon of charity
Turned to dust.

But in the grey light of this December
My thoughts were drawn again,
To last year's stab of conscience.
Back to the freezing rain.
To the ones we've clambered over
At the bottom of the pile where it hurts
Under our combined well fed weight,
To claim our just deserts.
Sleigh bells and fake snow nudge me
As paralysed, lost and listless
The ghosts of poverty haunt me
'Coz homelessness only happens at Christmas.
 I still had that Nordic sleeping bag.
Just handling it took me back,
Her essence, an image I couldn't have made.
And a spectre, though I tried, I couldn't evade.
I found myself back on that street,
With sleeping bag in hand, I stood.
Near that shop, still boarded up
A skeletal face looked from under his hood,
His glance slapped me like a cold wet hand.
Eyes front, I strode on past as best I could
Straight past, clutching that bag,
Head confused, appalled.
My still, small voice was banging on
But not so still and not so small.

cont.

"Breathe. What was I fearing?"
Through the steamed up window of Costa peering,
The world and his credit card rushing past.
"What was I thinking!"
Behind the counter, cutlery plinking.
Super-dry boys in wet denim, drinking,
The noise, the clatter, the nonsense the clinking
And all the while, my fortitude shrinking.

Marching now, guided by Google,
Dizzy with caffeine and driven by scruples.
To a drop-in, a shelter. A refuge near Splott,
So I went in ...I just went in.
But once inside, I froze to the spot.

As voices carried through the air,
With essence of Bisto, Detol and drying wet hair.
A face appeared before me:
   "You ok?" She asked, grey hoodie, shaved head.
   "I'm actually looking for someone I saw last year" I said,
"In a doorway next to Marks".
   She turned away. "Right", she replied. "I'll find you someone to ask".

I scanned the church hall:
Trestle tables with tea urns,
Where unshaven, stooped men
And frozen women took turns.
Volunteers in hi vis
Tell a police officer how it is.
And bundles of clothes,
Neat piles of the nation's
Discarded creations.
Organized formations
At various work stations
From so many locations.
Essential curations,
Of endlessly, endlessly, precious donations.
..."Were you looking for someone?" A suited man appeared
Young, with a name badge and trendy, trimmed beard.
"A homeless girl, I'm told", he says. He asks me my name.
I give him my details, he writes them down,
And repeats them back the same.

cont.

Rob Kersley

I tell him, now somewhat defensive,
He makes notes, I try to read ...apprehensive.
I tell him my story, garbled and now trembling,
Chapters and verses and all a bit rambling.

Then a voice from behind me: "Yes, I think I remember".
The same girl in the hoodie is squinting at me.
"Last year wasn't it?" says a young face, pale and slender.
"I'd been on the streets for a while,
Must have been late in December.
I ran, I'm sorry. I was scared.
I didn't trust anyone.
It was not long after that, that I woke up in a hospital bed.
With tubes and monitors and bright lights.
They caught me, then this place saved me.
They got me a flat and I help out here.
The money's crap, but the customers are the best." She laughs.

I hand her that sleeping bag at last.
   "Someone's gonna so appreciate this." She says.
Then, for a few seconds she froze.
 ...Bright blue, young eyes smiling,
That could have so easily closed.

Sleepless In November

May - she doesn't really love me,
Farrell - he doesn't need to tackle safely.
Corbyn - he should pretend no more,
His certain immunity from the law.
Millions. More despairing than Cameron would know,
Afforded to number tens on shirts as pure, as driven snow.
Two pay cheques from eviction, roll a loaded dice.
In that monolith to dominance, and waxed-jacketed birthrights.
While millionaire politicians claim, "We're all in this together."

Sleepless in the darkest November,
Repairing to dismember.
On shuffle, in a muddle:
Baited by scandalous audacity,
Of blow by blow atrocities.
Am I the sole witness
In a tale of treason and tragedy?
Paranoiac, trapped, insomniac.

Half-dreaming, dark-streaming
From fridge to tablet.
Cold chicken chow mein, to live newsfeed
Binging at 3:00am.
But be careful what you feed that brain.
Swallow, digest - repeat,
In the end you become
What you eat.

Rob Kersley

Don't Let Go

Sometimes, when she's good there's peace.
Like oil poured onto her troubled bay
As her gales cease.

Sometimes, when his tired eyes smile,
That tremor in his pale cheek
Is banished for a while.

Sometimes, when her shoulders calm,
That tormented spring uncoils.
And she unties her arms.

Sometimes, (but not today) he's good,
And these harsh rhymes and reasons
Are somehow understood.

For today, she stumbles again
Through dark forests, tight with trees,
Barbed briars and bracken.

Or swimming through a swirling
Throng of kelp. Endless, exhausting,
Clinging and whirling.

This is overload on a muscle,
Not a bicep or hamstring,
But a central, sensory tussle.

This is sickness of an organ,
But not kidneys or liver or heart
Or skin or lung.

To the world, he's exhausting,
They see an anger, confusion,
Distance, aggression.

They see no illness, no reason,
No possible justifiable
Explanation.

cont.

Rob Kersley

No scar, no limp, no crutch, no sling
To evoke sympathy, patience
Or any such thing.

She's plain miserable, so terse.
Tolerated at best,
But excluded at worst.

He's drowning before your eyes,
His motherboard shorting,
His electrodes misfiring.

And all she sees and all she hears,
Every comfort of every word,
Somehow only serves to reinforce her worst fears.

They, are one in just four of us
Who'll be afflicted with this illness
This coming year.

Take their hand and don't let go.
Become their rock ...they need you more
Than you both know.

Domestically Abused

Door unlocked,
Coat dropped.
Clogs popped,
Sofa flopped.
Late home ...crocked.

She's done her best with his tortilla stack,
Delivered to his disapproving lap.
The sigh he heaves
She chooses to believe,
Is appreciation.

Her appearance tired,
Less frequently inspired,
Motivation misfired.
What once was vibrant
Now timid, compliant.

Self-confidence systematically undermined,
So that she is only worthy
When he decides.
He: The sole opinion,
The sole arbiter.

The sole dispenser of currency,
Tossing her occasional morsels.
She grows to quietly hate herself
For her dependence.

His template for control:
Fear, suspended suspense,
Unpredictable bursts of offence,
Confusion and layered deceitful pretence.
She's sickened by the rumours,
From which he no longer manoeuvres.

The Mid-Terms today,
Her chance to break free.
But in her current state of mind
She's not going anywhere,
And tragically, they're both aware.

cont.

Rob Kersley

Her fifty states once empowered,
That happy Star Spangled flower.
Her Uncle Sam's niece,
Reduced now, to this.
The corrupted Liberty Belle,
On a Club Class flight to Hell.

Time and Space and Trewellard

Don't be fooled
By the relentless blue green swell,
As it crashes
On the Trewellard granite.

Enchanted as we are
By the tireless surge,
The endless, endless energy
Unstoppable rhythms,
Of this moody deep, deep ocean.

The tin miners were.
Their tired bodies,
Skin stained to a burnt ochre hide.
They saw a mirage of prosperity
That looked for all the world like eternity.
Lives seemed in harmony
With their ocean.
As bare hands harvested the ore.

The New Year was 1839, when over 7000 children
Were employed in Cornish mines.
When twelve was one year too young
To go underground.
Children and women worked above,
Breaking rocks with a hammer.
All before the union of Europe
And their fussy regulations and red tape
Of working conditions
And minimum wages.

Summer and winter
Men and teenagers climbed down homemade ladders,
A hundred or so feet,
Into darkness, dust and fumes.
These Cornish miners had to buy their own
Tools, candles and dynamite.
High fatality rates at the precarious, cramped, red hot rock face.
To emerge bent double
And squinting at the sparkling blue horizon,
Or bowed before the slate grey Atlantic

As they trudged back to their homes.

1839, one hundred years before the 2nd
Of two World Wars of unthinkable carnage.
With just twenty one years between them.
Only one hundred and eighteen years
Before that first union of Europe was formed
With their fussy regulations and red tape
A key aim, to bring peace at last to the region.

Don't be fooled by this
Spinning ancient rock.
Suspended in space,
Fixed by a magnetic gravity
Amidst a universe,
Distant. Disinterested in our bickering.
Freezing, endless, timeless, blackness.

Our only home:
It looks like it could spin forever.
Beneath our watchful moon pulling the tides.
Our garden since the first dawn,
Harvested, quarried, stripped.

Driven by need,
Blinkered by hunger.
Then blinded by the reflection
Of coins.
In our Ray Bans
With our mountains of stuff.

Every hammer
And every drill.
Every cart
Pulled by every pony.

Every furnace, every foundry.
Every engine, every factory.
Every pylon, every container.
Every tanker, every landfill.
Invests nothing in her.

cont.

Don't believe this doesn't hurt her,
That she doesn't flinch with the scars.
That she doesn't shudder in her sleep,
Doesn't choke as she roasts under the sun.

Her youthful barrier reef
The first symptom.
Her seas clogged with plastic,
Ice caps receding.
Clocks ticking
More loudly,
More urgent than ever.
Ambitious emissions targets set,
Expensive new plant, huge investment
Imposed upon itself by the union of Europe
For others to follow.
Such fussy regulation and red tape.
Wasted profits some might say.
De-regulate,
De-regulate,
De-regulate.
'Cos Tommy says he wants his *sovrunty back*.
And MPs want his vote.
So as long as the tail wags the dog,
Tommy will get what Tommy wants
And Tommy is not forced
To face up to his future
...Or his past.

Make hay while stocks last
And keep your head down.
Make out that we'll live forever.
But don't be fooled,
That we or she ever could.

"We cannot aim at anything less than the Union of Europe as a whole, and we look forward with confidence to the day when that Union will be achieved."- Sir Winston Churchill.

Rob Kersley

When You Look at Me That Way

The other day, that squall blew through,
We came in from our walk,
And then you looked at me that way.
I know you want to talk.

What was on your fathomless mind?
There's something wrong, I know.
What words, what note could you not find?
Oh please, just tell me so.

Because ever since then, I've been
Turning inside and out.
Going round and round in circles,
What was that all about?

Or perhaps I already see,
Like your deep chestnut eyes.
Touching the raw essence of me
Where only truth resides.

Do you believe I can fix this?
Your confidence misplaced.
You wait and stare expectantly,
Such faith, so pure, so chaste.

The years, they've been so kind to you
...So very kind to us.
And fifteen times seven ...a good age,
We're in floods of gratefulness.

I'll do what I can and Liz will too
Every day. But please, I pray:
My dearest, dearest, dearest friend,
Don't look at me that way.

A Game of Many Halves

Half the shirts in Cardiff will be white,
Half the shirts in the pubs will be red.
Half the defence will be Celtic,
Half the invasion will be Saxon.
Half the futility will be resisted,
Half the resistance will be futile.
Half the blood will be red,
Half the air will be blue.

Half the Welsh baby boys will be named,
Justin, or Jonathan, or Josh,
Half the Welsh baby girls will be named,
Gareth, or Alun, or Ken!

Half of Farrell's tackles will be illegal,
Half of Liam's ...suicidal.
Liam:
Half JPR, half Sella, half Cullen, half Blanco
Half gazelle, half emu, half shaman,
Never half-hearted.

Half the chariots will need roadside assistance,
Half the Delilahs will laugh no more.
Half of the land will be that of my Father's
Half of the bread will be the product of heaven.

Half tattoo, half skin,
Half kith, half kin.
Half man, half beer,
Half hope, half fear.
Half skill, half luck,
Half leap, half duck.

We were half plastered in Paris,
Then half rumbled in Rome.
But it's a game of many halves
When we get England at home!

Rob Kersley

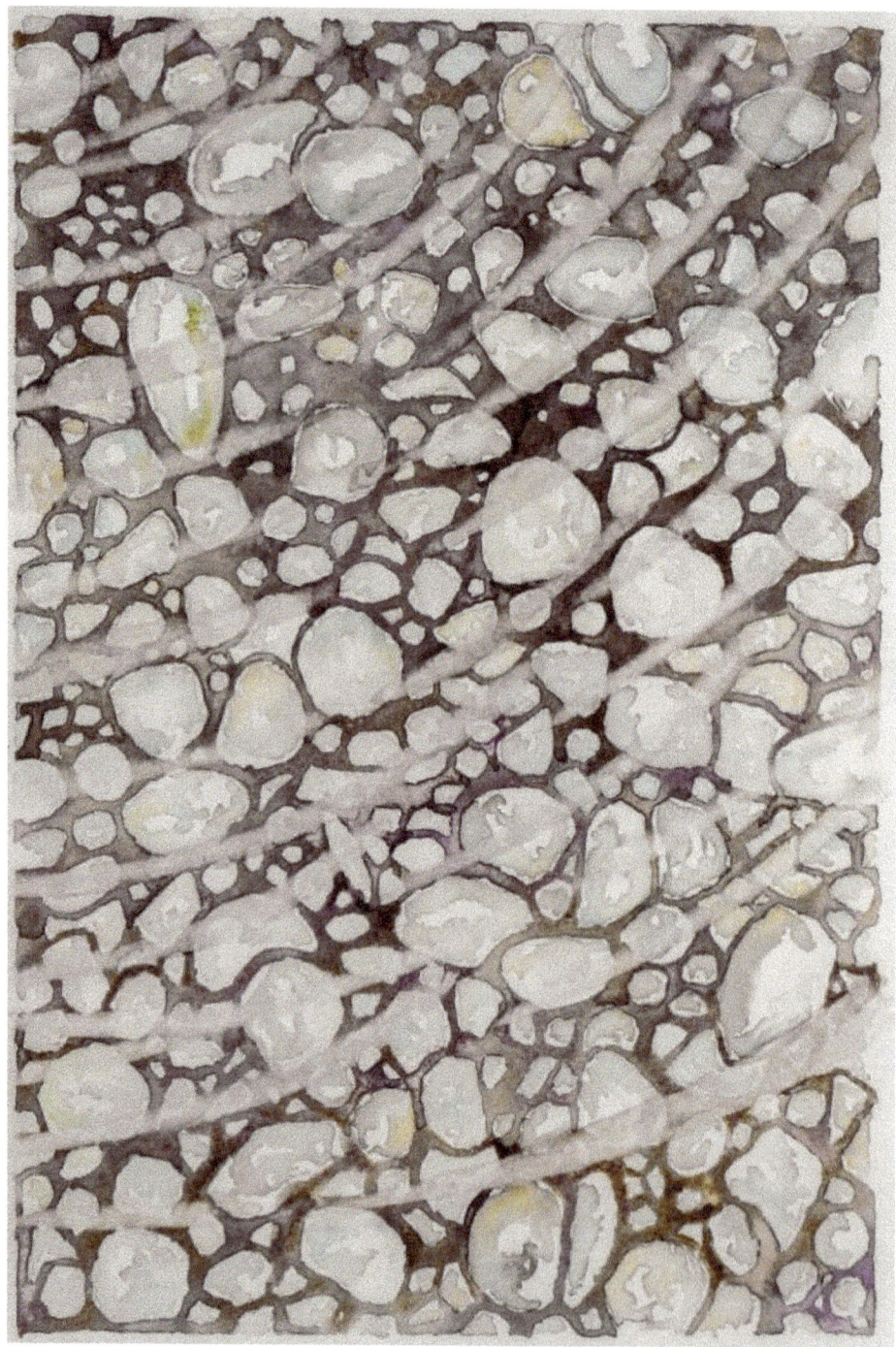

Tickled Trout

Us trout, we never learn.
Never question the insincere caress,
Or think beyond
Those soothing strokes.

Such banality as to becalm
Such simple, timid, creatures as us.
Soothed
To a vacant stupor.

Mouths open,
Eyes glazed.
Weary from an age of effort,
Worn down by the struggle
Of simply swimming against this endless tide.
Pushing against the heavy volume.
Willing, so willing to be mesmerized,
By the dancing, swaying weeds
And rotating shafts of light
That play like slowly revolving searchlights
Intruding into our dimmed, insulated solitude,
In the only perspective that exists:
The crisp, glinting current.
The past: Just a story told, soon forgotten,
Lost forever downstream
Along with its endeavour, its sacrifice and its pain.
A history that never happened
No lessons there to learn.

The steady press of the flow,
Distorts our peripheral view to a watery blur.
So the only clarity
Is that most narrow corridor of vision.
Our split screen of focus only aligns the image
Through our single point of reference.
No unexpected enlightenment then,
Just our intended object of attention.
And in it, we see exactly what we expected to see.
Perpetual reinforcement
Of those cherished preconceptions,

cont.

Just as we anticipated.
Just as we suspected.

We trout,
Weary from the effort
Welcome those comforting touches,
When they come
From that other world above the surface,
A world away from ours.
And even when accompanied,
By unnerving nudges and prods
The attention, the distraction is an uneasy relief.
Then…
Jolted into confusion.
Contradictions, contrition of constitution.
An unease. A basic fear from which they promise sincerely to protect.
When inexplicably,
We find ourselves gasping on the bank,
Essentials withheld at their pleasure, we strain rigid, gulping as a reflex,
Dispassionately observed, as we choke.

Until, with an effortless
Flick of the wrist, stroke of the pen, click of the mouse,
We're saved. Spared. Trembling. Terrified.
Grateful to be back in harness,
Promising devotion to this master,
Pledging allegiance to some flag.
Swearing obedience to a monster,
Safe again within the confines
Of his negotiated borders.

Those staring eyes that peer down through the ripples of our pool.
Those fingertips that lure and coax and caress.
Those words that flatter and inflame and stupefy.
And the trout:
Both his morsel and his means.

Lamorna

She was in one of her quiet moods yesterday,
Reflective, like a perfect mirror.
Not a breath, those wrinkles …gone,
Tranquility between the storms.

She's watched them come and go,
And with motherly patience,
In her caressing cove,
She cradles her own.

How many pebbles does she hold,
How perfect the image, the texture, her tones.
And what harmony
In the safe circle of those countless fragments.

I picked one up,
It lay, so heavy in my hand.
Irregular, asymmetric,
Beautifully flawed, random and unique
As every passing soul.
Perfectly shaped by its life in that place,
As ancient as time.

The fabric of Lamorna,
In transit over a galaxy of years.
Like small moons,
Eroding imperceptibly
To egg-shaped forms,
And finally to the pale, glinting sand
That returns in the end
To be washed.
Soothed to sleep
By her tender shore.

IKEAworld

Perhaps I fell in love too soon.
Unexpectedly swept off my feet,
Caught unawares,
As I was.
As we were,
Entering IKEAworld.

Was it the organized storage,
The coordinated fabrics,
The products, known by their designer's names,
The displays, a glimpse of that utopian IKEAworld.

The philosophy:
An advanced existence,
Of sustainability,
Durability,
Buildability,
Affordability
Synchronicity,
The next level of IKEAworld.

I followed the arrows marking the pathway.
Drifted with the procession,
The enlightened,
The forward thinkers,
The Evian drinkers,
At ease,
At home in IKEAworld.

With my little IKEA pencil,
Scribbling on my list.
Photos with my phone,
Item numbers and details, you know
Like all the others were,
Technology harnessed at last in IKEAworld.
Tolerance harvested,
Dreams of the civilized,
Reached out and realized in IKEAworld.

cont.

Rob Kersley

They have a restaurant,
Those genius IKEA folk.
'Meatball Meal' - £2.99
None of your regular rubbish mind
Intelligent meatballs,
For discerning, more considered appetites.
Yes, smart meatballs,
Yet, surprisingly high quality meatballs.
The cleverest meatballs,
For this cleverest, cleverest nation of IKEAworld.
Notice how everyone
Is strangely sedated,
Quietly animated
And curiously calmed by
This overwhelming wonderland
Of Formica.
Young families, speechless
Before the vision
Of how perfect life can be.
Shoes, displayed in an actual shoe rack
...And all of them, the right way up.
...And all of the laces are undone, how very sensible
(but what would you expect)
In the soft-close drawer,
Of a light-oak effect wardrobe.
A fantasy of perfection
In chipboard.
A teasing glimpse of the many, many possibilities,
Of IKEAworld.

Imagine, that level of order.
Just imagine, that degree of non-clutter.
Dare to dream,
As you follow the stream.
That this life
...could be your life.
Where organised meets style,
Where economy meets design.
Where modesty meets intelligence,
Where tolerance meets the home,
Where harmony meets the family.

                                                                                         cont.

I turned around and reached out
In a single movement.
Glazed over
Still gazing over my shoulder
At the cushions.
But my trolley (my still empty trolley)
Was gone.
It was there
It was right there, I could have sworn!
Who takes someone else's trolley?

I found another,
Suspected to have been abandoned,
By my trolley thief.
And it's not the end of the world,
But I don't like it as much as mine,
With its grubby handle ...a bit sticky,
And its clunking wheel that pulls it to the left
Always pulling to the damned left.

I scanned soft furnishings,
Searching for the villain,
Increasingly flushed, heated, angry.
And in my way are stupid families
With their stupid children
Stopped dead in the stupid aisle,
Like stupid sheep in a stupid lane.
Gawping at the stupid displays.
And stupid elderly people
In their stupid clothes,
Dawdling at a stupid snail's pace.
All of them in my way,
In a conspiracy to ruin my life,
As I marched and scanned,
Fuming, raging,
For a sight of that villain,
For a sight of the cause of my angst.

Steering this stupid trolley,
The faults of which are not my fault.
This state I'm in is not my fault.
And all I can see is cheap furniture

cont.

Rob Kersley

And all I can taste is meatballs.
And all I can think about is revenge.

All I can hear are strange accents
They only come here to steal,
Looking for handouts
Pinching our trolleys.
They're everywhere,
But the really bad ones
Like the one I'm after ...is evasive,
Crafty, slippery, dangerous.
Yes, they are
Very dangerous.

Just get me out of here,
Can't be doing with this,
This flat-pack charade,
I want to be home.
I take a short cut to overtake the masses.
Through a small doorway in bedding,
Only to emerge all the way back
In sofas.

I'll ask an assistant, but it turns into a tirade,
'…and while you're about it you can cancel my IKEAworld store card
because I can assure you,
I'm never coming back.
Although …I hope I'll still get the discount when I buy online
And I assume you'll still notify me of special offers,
It's the least you can do,
After all the money I've spent
After the life I dreamt of,
Is now in tatters.'

Get me out of this mess,
All I want is to leave this blue and gold block,
Its perfection required too much of me.
Its aspirations, unrealistic anyway.
Take me home to my cul-de-sac,
Back to my telly,
To my clutter.

cont.

Get me back behind my door,
Keep them out.
Cos there's us, and there's them,
And IKEAworld,
…That was just an illusion.

Culture Check

A cold, stiff figure,
Dead wings in frozen rigor.
Pineapple claws like clenched fists
As it was, braced for its sad mortis.

Carried in the jaws of a Brecon Bobtail,
Strutting through a mid-December deluge,
When confronted by another,
Observing, tracking this bedraggled mother.

First, the stand-off,
The circling.
First to blink,
These two had been waiting for this.

Then a howling, ancient screech.
And locked, tumbling,
Furious, fearless fighting. Fur flying.
Bystanders standing by, engrossed, shocked, personifying.

Still clutching that long dead starling in her jaws,
Fending off that mugger with little more than clawed paws.
Spilling down the flooded street,
For dear life, through the shoppers, and cold wet leaves.

On and on it went,
Until, breathless and bleeding he gave up.
And to that poor dead thing, she clung,
In defiant dignity. In denial but beaten, visibly.

Then, from behind St Mary's they emerged:
An endless, rising cloud of birds.
Massing, dancing. A swaying symphony,
A murmuration, a visual cacophony.

For disconnected humans,
To look up for a moment
From their isolated ruts.
Made something else by the endless carnage,
Playing out in the gutters of this land.

cont.

To glimpse some culture lost.

Is there hope, if we recognize such cryptic symbols?
As thousands of tiny, modest creatures,
A collective, spontaneous impulse.
Celebrating unity.
Instinctive and with such certainty.
A massed choir
Of joy and harmony.

Rob Kersley

Long Rock Landmark

My first memory?
...Not sure,
Nothing explicit, but there was excitement.
Not certain, but I smelled freshly cut grass somewhere.
I remember now,
Looking up at flowers as tall as oaks against an endless, cornflower sky.
Laughter from somewhere, as I found my feet,
Music playing, as I fell asleep
And woke to smiling faces watching,
Faces I would etch into my heart.
The ones I could trust,
The ones I would protect
As my role became clearer
And I filled that loose fitting skin.

My first thought?
...You've asked me this before
And I couldn't answer.
But I see now that you mean something of your world.
Your busy days of planning
And creating,
Forever striving.
For me, I just feel,
And feeling is all I feel.
But what I feel is true, it's real.
I know myself well, in this mellow evening of my life,
And welcome these familiar feelings as they visit me now.
None are ever too far away,
But they don't surprise me as they used to.

Yes, what a week.
You baked a cake, topped with candles on Monday,
Helped me into the car on Tuesday.
And we walked over a bank of crispy, crunching kelp
And ever so quietly into that soft, whispering, swaying water
That squeezed my toes into the familiar sand.
Sweet salt on the warm, spring Marazion breeze,
As the sparkling light danced all around us.

cont.

Rob Kersley

Then we visited those people in that building:
They ate your cake.
I recognized the disinfected fingers
Of the soft hands that stroked me.
Patient eyes, hands on olive, tunicked hips,
Smiling down at me, incredulous.
In that place that took the pain away,
Just a few moons ago,
When the biting easterly blew the scattering, grey birds from the sky.
When I couldn't stand,
Couldn't eat.
You held me.
Through the heavy odour,
Like an aftertaste on every breath, fear.
...And you wouldn't let go.

Yes, I'm good again now.
Fifteen you say
...What does that mean?

How long is this journey anyway,
And when did it all start?
Can we go back there?
...I hope so.

The Fast Bubble

Old-timers would call it a *fast bubble*.
Old-timers, in bib and braces,
Stained tweed cap
With busy eyes behind sawdust hazed spectacles.

Old-timers whose hands of polished hide
Marked dovetails with a razor blade.
Possessive of their Cascamite formulae,
Sufficiently, secretively vague
Over critical joinery details,
And second fix fixations.

Their most precious instrument of precision:
Their *fast bubble* spirit level.
Cosseted, coveted.
Protected in its prescriptive,
Handmade,
Velvet-lined,
Piano hinged,
Rosewood case.

His reputation after all,
Reliant on such fundamental foundations.
His pride of obsessive workmanship,
Defined by accuracy, to be ingrained as his legacy.
He entrusts all this to a bubble;
The fastest, of fast little bubbles.

The fast bubble
Rests centrally, only
When at absolute equilibrium.
The fast bubble
Responds with immediacy to the merest hint of deviation,
Diving this way and that,
In the very narrowest of vials
Of highly polished, engineered glass,
To indulge the slippery, jittery bubble
In its tantalizing tango,
Of absolute,
Precision based,

cont.

Rob Kersley

Zero tolerance accuracy.

My exhausting, *fast bubble* …I could well do without!
Seldom centred,
Scarcely settled,
Stridently satisfied,
In alerting me to a fraction of imbalance.
A siren to the most marginal of inconsistencies.
A forewarning of the dreaded, impending, double standard.

Why can't mine be a forgiving, *slow bubble*?
Relaxed, reclined and rotund
In sun hat and shades and flowery shorts.
Lolling in an inflatable ring
With drinks holders
Holding cocktails,
In tall glasses
With umbrellas.
Stabled in a generous, glass tube
With a barely detectable upward arc
To steady, a contentedly comfortable centrally biased bubble.
Just soaking up the sun,
...Y'know,
Chillin' wid da boyz,
By the pool.
Going with the flow.

No, not mine!
Not mine, the barely awakened
Static, stationary, stable sanctuary.
Not mine, the slow bubble of peacefully accepting disharmony.

Mine will pull away to the right
At the slightest whiff.
Before I've even noticed
That we're
(Getting close to being),
(Not too far from),
(If we're not very careful),
(Not entirely),
On the level.
Before the discord of unease

                                                            cont.

Has made itself heard,
My precious little fast bubble will fly off to the left.
Or the moment before I think:
I've said too much,
Or too little,
Not enough,
...It's too late.

However,
There are moments.
Not rare, but priceless moments,
When that bubble is held steady, dead centre.
When the planets become realigned,
When shoulders ease and lungs again can breathe,
As her patient, blue green eyes pull me back home.
I've no idea how she calms that trembling little fast bubble of mine,
I'm just grateful that she does.

They Can Come Out Now

It's ok.
The coast is clear,
They can come out now.
Open the concealed hatch,
And lead your daughters
From the cellar.

It's ok, they can come out now,
He's returned back to that other place,
His business trip completed.
Eyeing his next acquisition,
Luring his prey from the circle of gold-starred wagons.
Meeting with the traitors.
Salivating over the possibilities.

Yes, it's ok they can come out now,
Lead them back into the sunshine.
Your monarchs doffed their cowardly caps.
Your leaders licked the cowboy boots
And stood side by side in remembrance
Of the tragic sacrifices made
To halt an ego-maniac,
A corrupt fascist, with global ambitions.
Point out the irony to your daughters,
Once they've adjusted to the light.

Because it's ok,
They can come out now.
He's lumbering back to his Vegas empire,
To his symbolically tacky, fake gold tower,
An obscenity of his gross misuse of power.
To kneel once more at the altar of greed,
An insatiable appetite to feed.

They can come out now,
The coast is clear,
For a while, a lighter atmosphere.
Rest assured for now. Relax,
But keep that cellar warm.

cont.

Because rest assured,
He will be back,
For this,
Is his perfect storm.

Rob Kersley

Tug of Love

All he can see,
Is the top of a baseball cap,
Peak facing back.
Face bowed as ever, lit by a screen.
All he can see in his rear view mirror,
As he goes through the gears,
Fast forward through the years
That led to the split.
Of man and woman,
Of family home,
And a tug of love for the solitary, salvageable solace,
Of a life, once complete.
Wordless, distant,
Slouched now,
On the back seat.

Indulged by both estranged, beleaguered parents,
Like an arms race
Of clothes and gadgets and holidays,
Of everything he doesn't need.
For little Anglik, this tug of love
Has become his currency,
For as long as he can remember.
Instinctively manoeuvring as he does,
Manipulating as he does,
Accumulating as he does.
Trading as he does,
Just enough to suggest
Approval without commitment,
Forgiveness for the moment at least,
Allegiance without the burning of bridges.

Not the most straightforward of times,
And this, a strange three way tussle.
For one parent's recent ex-partner, with no right.
Him, of all people ...blatantly,
Unashamedly reckless in his suggestions
Of liberation.
The vaguest hint of a legacy,
Of an entitlement to entitled little Anglik.

cont.

Rob Kersley

Had Mum and Dad got on,
Had Mum and Dad talked,
Had Mum and Dad shown integrity,
Had their language so offensive
Not made Mum and Dad so defensive,
Then they might have acted in Anglik's best interests.
Then the serpent in his clammy,
Scaly coat of Tweed
Would have been exposed indeed,
Sent away.
His corrosive, venomous views
Rightfully consigned to a mere
Ugly, cold blooded passage of history.

Had Mum and Dad not had previous,
Had they not had old scores to settle, points to prove,
Then Anglik might have been saved.
But arguments forged of principal,
Distracted both parents from the seemingly implausible,
The apparently impossible.

Because instead, they tried to compete on his terms.
Instead, they gave credence to the usurper,
But fatally, they lacked his conviction,
Which, of course Anglik,
Demanding little Anglik saw through.
So when push came to shove,
Came to votes, came to power…
Suddenly, unbelievably,
Amid the imminent danger that Anglik still fails to see,
That, posed by the snake with nothing to offer,
With nothing of substance on which to draw
Stifling Anglik's growth,
Corrupting young Anglik's impressionable soul,
Leading little Anglik into the shadows.
Dangerously thin ice from which the serpent's
Hidden, cannibalistic masters hope to profit.
…many years since the stakes have been this high.

One attribute of the serpent,
He's a communicator.
One truth of this smiling, laughing menace,

                                                                        cont.

He's an opportunist
Who identifies the vacuum,
Created by a struggle.
He recognises the space left
In the disharmony of these polarised parents,
And he focuses his subject upon it,
Without ever having to say exactly what that something is.
After all, that space will represent something different,
Something uniquely lost, to each and every viewer.
So why be specific,
When a sort of nostalgic reinvention,
Will fit whatever shaped void is left,
Between those warring factions.

Perhaps, we Angliks had this coming,
A white cliffs-shaped chip on our collective shoulders.
Perhaps, we Angliks have to go through this,
Having been raised on a sugary, fatty diet
Of arrogant superiority.
Then grinding our teeth
At the seemingly irretrievable ground lost
In the intervening years,
When we failed to learn some fundamental truths.
When we failed to remember some rudimentary life skills,
From short sighted leaders
In a twisted,
In an ultimately selfish, tug of love.
Yes, I think we had this coming.

Acknowledgements

Thank you to Mayar Akash who as publisher, has showed such generosity of patience, in giving me the opportunity, the focus and the self-belief to see this project through.

Also, a big Thank You to Michelle Blaken BA (Hons) PGCE for her painstaking attention to detail and professionalism of her artwork photography of my illustrations.

My eternal appreciation goes out to my wonderful family, the Brecon and South Wales communities, my friends at Coast FM and the entire readership of my pieces. Your warm and enthusiastic support has succeeded in coaxing me further and further along this road.

Finally, to my wife Liz; When words failed me, there you appeared.

About the Author

Rob Kersley was born in Usk, Wales and was educated at Wern Secondary Modern School and Mid-Gwent College, Pontypool. He worked as a carpenter/joiner, surveyor, manager, operations director and managing director before re-evaluating and re-training as a deep tissue therapist.

He then established himself as the sole practitioner of a well-respected and successful deep tissue therapy practice near Brecon from 2003 until 2018 before relocating with his wife Liz to Cornwall where his daughter had settled some years earlier.

He joined Coast FM in Penzance as a presenter in 2019 where he hosts a weekly radio show covering non-mainstream, contemporary artists and their music from around the globe. His poetry was first published in 2022, in version eight of Penny Authors. Having those poems published and seeing his work in print, woke an aspiration to publish his own books of art and poetry. This opportunity presented itself through Penny Authors, to fulfil a lifelong dream. This he seized, and this book is the first of many more to come.

www.ingramcontent.com/pod-product-compliance
Lightning Source LLC
Chambersburg PA
CBHW040929240426
43667CB00026B/2994